Launching the Church School Year

Joseph John Hanson
Kenneth D. Blazier

JUDSON PRESS, Valley Forge

LAUNCHING THE CHURCH SCHOOL YEAR

Copyright © 1972
Judson Press, Valley Forge, Pa. 19481

International Standard Book No. 0-8170-0553-6
Library of Congress Catalog Card No. 75-181558

Printed in the U.S.A.

Contents

Introduction

This manual is intended for use in churches by boards or committees of Christian education and the general superintendent of the church school in planning the opening, or the "Launch" of the church school year. The Launch at the start of the new school year includes the activities, processes, and events designed to get the church school under way effectively.

The board and the general superintendent are concerned for the effectiveness of the church school. The board demonstrates its concern through the policy it formulates in relationship to the school. The superintendent expresses his concern by implementing that policy in his administration of the church school. This manual suggests the use of the launching of the new year as a means of increasing the effectiveness of the church school. The suggestions here may be helpful to churches of many denominations and with any curriculum plan or resources.

This manual attempts to:

• focus upon the church school and its place in the educational ministry of the church.

• suggest emphases, practical program suggestions, and resources that will be helpful to boards of Christian education and church school workers in designing a relevant and meaningful annual Launch of the church school year.

• define roles of the board of Christian education, and in particular the church school superintendent, in relationship to the events of the annual Launch.

This manual—
- considers the significance of the Launch (Section 1).
- describes five major emphases for the Launch, and program options for each (Section 2):

*Planning for
teacher support
and training*
(Section 6)

Planned during Launch
and implemented
during the year

*Preparing
to minister with
students*
(Sections 4-5)

- Recruitment and preparation of leaders
- Enrollment
- Planning visitation program to be implemented during the year

*Celebrating
Launch Sunday*
(Section 7)

Events for the
kickoff Sunday of
church school
year

*Determining
objectives; policy
for church school year*
(Section 8)

by board of
Christian education

*Acquainting
the congregation
with the school*
(Section 12)

Interpretation of
significance of the
church school

- suggests steps in designing the Launch (Section 3).
- highlights Launch roles for:
  —the board of Christian education (Section 8).
  —the church school superintendent (Section 9).
  —the pastor (Section 10).
  —the church school staff (Section 11).

Section 1 Significance of the Annual Launch

The Launch of the church school year is significant because it offers an annual opportunity for churches to map out a strategy to increase the effectiveness of the teaching-learning opportunities within the church school.

The annual Launch is suggested as a way of beginning the new church school year with maximum effectiveness. It can be likened to the start of the public school year when parents get their children ready to go back to school, pupils are enrolled in their classes, teachers prepare for the new year, rooms are made ready, and an adequate supply of textbooks and other teaching-learning aids is provided for the coming year.

The suggested goals of the annual Launch are:

• to encourage members of the entire congregation to participate responsibly in the church school.

• to prepare learners and leaders of the church school for their roles in teaching-learning opportunities of the coming year.

• to celebrate the beginning of a new church school year.

Launching the church school year finds its significance as an annual emphasis designed to focus attention upon:

1.) *The church school in the context of the total ministry of the church*

The start of the new public school year includes the activities, processes, and events which get the school under way each September. Likewise, the Launch relates to a variety of educational activities in the church and to the launching of the church's total program of educational ministry for the year. This means that the events of the annual Launch of the church school:

• should be related to other educational events in the fall, such as a youth retreat or a school of missions.

• should highlight the church school *as part of* the church's educational program, but not as *the* total program.

• should emphasize the significance of the teaching ministry in undergirding the church's other ministries of proclamation, worship, fellowship, witness, and service.

2.) *Acquainting the constituency with opportunities for learning in the church school*

7

Because the church school is an ongoing program, it is easy to assume that everyone is familiar with its opportunities for teaching and learning. A more productive assumption may be that there are persons within the scope of the congregation who might participate in the church school if they were to be acquainted with the learning opportunities open to them.

3.) *The faculty of the church school*

A primary element in any teaching-learning situation is the teacher. A strategy of support and training of teachers is essential. The Launch of the church school year can be the occasion for development of such a strategy. (The strategy is then implemented during the school year.)

4.) *The church school objectives of the coming year*

The teaching-learning opportunities which are planned for classes or groups are designed to enable persons to become "aware of God through his self-disclosure, especially his redeeming love as revealed in Jesus Christ, and enabled by the Holy Spirit respond in faith and love." [1] The annual Launch affords an opportunity to take a new look at the implication of this overall objective.

Oliver Wendell Holmes is quoted: "I find the great thing in this world is not so much where we stand as in what direction we are moving." [2] Only when the leadership of a church school knows where they stand, and have defined in what direction they are planning to move, will they be able to evaluate their effectiveness. The launching of the church school year can be the occasion for defining achievable goals for the coming twelve months.

5.) *Celebration at the beginning of a new church school year*

Within the worship experiences of the church and the church school, persons may be afforded the opportunity to celebrate the potential in the coming year. This potential includes opportunities for discovery, growth, and the unfolding of persons during the interaction of learners, leaders, and the Holy Spirit within teaching-learning situations. Although celebration should be incorporated as a continual element within the life of the church school, the beginning of a new year of study can be something to be celebrated in a special way.

Some churches are seeking alternatives to the church school meeting on Sunday morning and in the church building. Examples

[1] *Foundations for Curriculum* (Valley Forge: American Baptist Board of Education and Publication, 1966), p. 13.

[2] Virginia Ely, *I Quote* (New York: George W. Stewart Publisher, Inc., 1947), p. 14.

suggested are after-school sessions, neighborhood groups for children or youth, and family clusters. The term "church school" is used in this manual to encompass the many efforts of churches to use the disciplines and structures of a *school* in providing regularly scheduled learning opportunities for persons of all ages. For some churches the "school" is held on Sunday morning in the church building. For other churches it is held at other times or in other places, or both. The annual Launch is related to all these churches.

Section 2 Major Areas of Emphasis in the Launch

The calendar of events in the annual Launch within the congregation will vary from year to year, depending upon the particular concerns to be highlighted at the beginning of the church school year.

Although certain emphases will undoubtedly be made each year, an emphasis may manifest itself in differing program elements. For example, while enrollment is essential at the outset of each year, enrollment as a program element may vary as to time, place, and procedures.

Five major areas of emphasis seem to be important for an effective launching of each church school year:

1.) *Determining objectives and policy for the year*

The board (or committee) of Christian education, in consultation with the church school superintendent, determines the objectives for the church school year. What do the board, superintendent, and other church school workers intend to accomplish in the coming year? In the spring, based on an evaluation of the present year, objectives should be proposed for the coming church school year, beginning in September. These objectives should be compatible with the other elements of the church's teaching ministry.

At the same time, policy decisions should be made by the board regarding such concerns as the selection and ordering of curriculum, budget, special days to be observed in special ways, and room assignments. These are administrative concerns to be given early consideration in the planning for the church school year.

This emphasis of the Launch is considered in more detail in Section 8, "Responsibility of the Board," and Section 9, "Role of the Church School Superintendent."

2.) *Preparing to minister with students*

After the formulation of objectives and policy some essential steps need to be taken to insure the possibility of effective teaching-learning opportunities within classes or groups. These steps include:

• the recruitment of the best qualified leaders for class and departmental groupings.

10

- the preparation of leaders for their roles.
- the enrollment of all possible persons for classes and groups of the school.
- the formulation of a program of visitation of students and prospective students. (The program is then implemented during the coming year.)

Sections 4 and 5 offer program options related to these steps.

3.) *Planning for teacher support and training*

Belonging to a supportive team may result in the more effective use of the leadership potential of a person. An annual concern of the Launch is the development of a strategy for building a sense of "teamness" among the workers of the church school. (The strategy is then implemented during the coming year.)

No one is ever fully trained as a teacher. An annual concern of the Launch is the planning of a training strategy to develop the teaching skills of teachers. (The strategy is then implemented during the coming year.) Section 6 suggests program options for teacher support and training.

4.) *Celebrating Launch Sunday*

On Launch Sunday the new church school year begins. This day is set aside to celebrate the new year and to challenge members of the congregation to participate responsibly in the teaching-learning groups of the church school. Section 7 suggests program options for this emphasis of the Launch.

5.) *Acquainting the congregation with the school*

The congregation needs to be informed concerning the objectives, life, and achievements of the church school. There is a need for a program of interpretation of what is happening in a church school and of the importance of congregational concern and involvement in this primary setting of the educational ministry of the church. Section 12, "Involving the Congregation," considers this emphasis of the Launch.

Section 3   Designing the Launch

The annual Launch represents much more than a conglomerate of unrelated happenings and programs. All program emphases within the total event should be designed to accomplish the goals of the annual Launch. (See page 7.)

A variety of possible programs and projects are described in this manual. Not all of these can be scheduled by every church, due to local circumstances and available leadership. But every church can accomplish some of these options, if the board is willing to take the time, make the preparation, and provide the leadership.

The task of designing the annual Launch should involve the entire board or committee of Christian education or a specially designated Launch Task Group in making decisions in relation to the following steps:

• State an overall goal.
• Explore all alternatives for reaching this goal.
• Select programs, projects, and emphases that can be accomplished.
• Organize to achieve each program.
• Calendar all events.
• Adopt a plan of evaluation.

If it is decided to assign the planning of Launch Sunday events to the general superintendent and a related task group, this decision should be finalized early each year, possibly in February, so that initial goal-setting, program determination, and designing can begin.

In selecting and designing a sequence of launch events the following questions ought to be considered:

• What were the positive and negative results of last year's Launch?
• Which emphases should be highlighted in the Launch? (See Section 2.)
• Which events should be scheduled again (or not repeated)? Why?
• What can be done to give the Launch an innovative, exciting dimension?

- How can more church school workers be involved?
- Who should design the launch events?

Answers to these basic questions will provide helpful data upon which to select the year's emphases and to assign program designing and administrative responsibility. In the course of this exploration, other relevant information may emerge. This information should be evaluated along with all accumulated data.

Many launch program ideas are included in this manual. Whoever designs the annual Launch should examine each of these to determine whether they are germane to the launch goal, and achievable in light of available time and leadership. Some boards may approve and adopt each suggested emphasis; others may choose one or two emphases specifically designed to undergird their educational ministry, church school, and teaching leadership.

Each of the launch emphases, following others in succession, creates a cumulative impact, focusing major attention upon the significance of Christian teaching in the church school, and the importance of individuals becoming involved in this aspect of the church's total ministry.

Having gathered and assessed the necessary data, the board or the Launch Task Group is in a position to take these further essential steps in designing the annual Launch:

1. *State an overall goal*

Consider the suggested goals of the annual Launch on page 2. These are specific objectives that can be achieved through a number of programs or projects. In selecting and designing launch events, this question should be asked of each: "Will this event help to accomplish a stated goal?" When the answer is clearly affirmative, the planning group is ready to move ahead.

Some boards or task groups may prefer to formulate their own goals. Each goal should be tested by such questions as:
- Is it achievable?
- Is it measurable?
- Is it based on reliable data?

2. *Explore all alternatives for reaching this goal*

In an open session for "idea sharing," encourage every board member to suggest possible ways of reaching each launch goal. Do not challenge each other's ideas. Record every suggestion on chalkboard or newsprint. At the end of this process, endeavor to group together similar ideas, to examine each one in relation to your goal statement, and to rank the suggestions in a priority sequence.

13

In addition, the board or task group will want to review the wide spectrum of program possibilities described in this manual. From these and the ideas from your "brainstorming" session, you may now identify priority programs and projects.

3. *Select programs, projects, and emphases that can be accomplished*

It is better to choose only a few than to select a large number which actually reflect "wishful thinking" and cannot be carried to a successful conclusion. Make certain that each program or event which is approved is reassessed in light of the stated goal. Endorse only those that are consonant with your overall launch goal.

In making priority program selections, consider all resources needed, including persons and time available, leadership capacities of board members and church school superintendent, response and support of all church school workers, and pastor's involvement and cooperation. If all of the leadership ability, strength, and commitment of these persons can be combined and focused upon events in the Launch, the chances of success are high indeed. *Actually, the key to success in program selection and implementation is "leadership."*

4. *Organize to achieve each program*

Determine the objective of each program so that everyone involved in the planning has a clear understanding of "what it is all about." Then select persons who are best qualified to take whatever "next steps" are necessary for further program development, implementation, staffing, and scheduling.

Throughout this process, however, those who have been delegated to design each program should maintain open channels of communication for the sharing of plans and the prevention of duplication. In addition, all plans being made for launch events should be shared regularly with members of the board for review and concurrence.

5. *Calendar all events*

The scheduling is almost as important as the selection of events. There are advantages in careful, intelligent calendaring, namely:

• Sufficient time between events encourages and enables members of the congregation as well as students to be more generous in attendance and response.

• A competent leader often can be involved in more than one important assignment.

• Administration is enhanced when programs follow in an uncrowded sequence.

- Conflicting programs can be identified and corrected before serious conflicts develop.

6. *Adopt a plan of evaluation*

Throughout the entire process of designing the annual Launch, the board members should keep in mind the principle and practice of "continuing evaluation" as an essential part of good programming. At every major step in the designing process, basic assumptions should be rechecked; objectives and goals assessed; new data examined; resources, including leadership, appraised; teacher and student responses tested; emerging plans for related programs or projects compared and evaluated. Helpful suggestions concerning evaluation procedures can be found in Section 12 of *Shaping the Church's Educational Ministry* by Kenneth L. Cober. (See Appendix B.)

Following the annual Launch, members of the board should allocate an adequate period of time for the assessment of "accomplishments," "failures," and "new learnings," recording these for guidance in the designing of subsequent launch events.

Materials: Those who plan launch events should be mindful of available program resources and of new curriculum materials that will be needed for orientation and training sessions for teachers. Appendix B of this manual contains an annotated bibliography of some resources.

Section 4 Recruitment and Preparation of Leaders

One emphasis in launching the church school year is the preparation for ministry with the learners in the teaching-learning opportunities. From the perspective of leadership this emphasis includes the recruitment and preparation of leaders for their roles. From the perspective of students the emphasis includes the enrollment of persons in classes or groups and the planning of the visitation program for the church school year.

The *planning* of a visitation program for the year is suggested as an essential launch element. That is, an effective launching of the church school year includes mapping out the visitation strategy, whereas that strategy may be implemented throughout the year.

In this section will be found program options related to:
• Recruitment of church school leaders
• Preparation of church school leaders

The next section will include suggestions for:
• Enrollment of persons in classes
• Visitation program

These are offered as options, from which you may choose the items which promise to enrich your launch experience or which may spark your creativity in formulating your own program possibilities in these areas.

RECRUITMENT OF CHURCH SCHOOL LEADERS

The *purpose* of the recruitment of church school leaders is to secure the best qualified persons to serve as teachers, superintendents, and officers of the church school in a given church school year.

Several guidelines are suggested here for the recruitment of leaders:

• *Leaders should be recruited before the school year begins.* Because the relationships between teachers and learners are of utmost importance, teachers should be recruited early enough to begin their responsibilities in the first session of the school year in the fall. Otherwise, some of the value of the initial sessions in terms of their contribution to future sessions will be lost.

• *The recruitment of church school leaders is an annual event.*

All leaders are probably best recruited to serve for the given period of the church school year. Some potential leaders are reluctant to accept positions of leadership because of an unwritten but understood assumption that once they become teachers, they are always teachers. Recruitment for a year at a time affords opportunities for an occasional leave of absence for teachers for a year or two, for recruiting an individual for a different position for the coming year, or for a dissatisfied or unqualified teacher to resign.

• *The church school teaching assignment should be regarded as the major responsibility of each teacher for the year.* The roles of church school leaders are major roles requiring considerable time and effort. The significance of one's responsibility is enhanced when that person is freed from other tasks in the church in order to spend major time in that responsibility.

• *The recruitment of church school leaders is dependent upon a continuing program of training of potential leaders.* Such a program involves potential leaders in training opportunities in which they may explore their capabilities and interest in different kinds of service and in which they may enhance skills or develop new skills. This program is a major concern of a chairman of leader development of the board of Christian education, in cooperation with the church school superintendent. Such training may include events within the local church and conferences or laboratory schools sponsored by a denominational or ecumenical group for a cluster of churches.

Possible steps in the recruitment of church school leaders are:

1.) *Determine the leadership required for the church school in the coming year.* A listing is needed (by grades and departments) of the positions to be filled, such as teachers, superintendent, and others.

2.) *State clearly what is desired of the person selected for each position.* What will you look for in a person who is to fill each position? The person will need to serve as a representative of the Christian community within the class or department and to help the school achieve its specific goals and overall objective of helping all persons "be aware of God in his self-disclosure" and "respond in faith and love." In addition, there is a need to describe the special qualifications of the leader to be secured for each position. A written job description is a helpful tool in recruiting leadership.

3.) *Discover potential leaders for the positions to be filled.* Perhaps a special task group, including the general superintendent, should be appointed by the board of Christian education to discover new prospects for leadership. A careful study of the church and church school rolls as well as conversations with key leaders and others in the church may enlarge the list of potential leaders. New members of the church should be carefully considered.

4.) *Select and invite the person most suitable for each job.* The approach should be planned carefully. The approach to a prospective leader may best be made by more than one person, perhaps someone representing the church as a whole, such as the pastor or chairman of the board of Christian education, and someone representing the age group or department where leadership is needed, such as a teacher or departmental superintendent. The potential leader should be given time to consider prayerfully the invitation extended to him, and not be pressed to respond immediately. It may be important for the person to speak with other members of the family in considering the invitation. A second visit may be required.

PREPARATION OF CHURCH SCHOOL LEADERS

The *purpose* of the preparation of church school leaders is to enable teachers, superintendents, and other leaders to be (1) familiar with the various resources available for their use and (2) knowledgeable about and involved in administrative policies and procedures related to their roles.

Four possibilities are suggested for the preparation of church school leaders. In a given year a church may undertake each of these possibilities as four steps in the preparation of leaders. In another year a church may elect one or more of these possibilities as a part of their design of launch events. The suggested possibilities are:

1.) *A retreat for church school staff*

Some churches have discovered that at least once a year all persons involved in the teaching ministry of the church school need to be together to clarify goals, to identify the learnings that have come in the past year, to project new plans, and to build a sense of oneness and concern for the persons reached in the ministry of the church school. For these reasons a retreat for the church school staff is suggested.

This kind of experience requires time. The retreat is scheduled in most churches in May or June in order to accomplish its basic purposes of review of the past year and planning for the future. A September retreat may be wise in some churches, offering opportunities for developing plans for the coming church school year with the newly recruited staff.

A variety of schedules are possible, including:
- a weekend (Friday evening through Sunday afternoon).
- two consecutive Saturdays or Sundays (morning-afternoon or afternoon-evening).
- two or three consecutive weekday evenings. (7–10 P.M.)

The retreat may include the total teaching staff of the school including teachers, superintendents, and persons giving leadership in art, music, and other specialized areas. Members of the board of Christian education and its committees should be included.

Departmental meetings may be desired during the retreat, for evaluation, planning, and dealing with specific concerns. The annual study theme or themes of the church school may be presented by the pastor or some other qualified person. Some study time may be included in the retreat to enable teachers to deal with the appropriate concepts and areas. A retreat affords the opportunity for an emphasis on team-building experiences in departmental groups and with the total teaching staff. (See Section 6.)

2.) *Distribution of resources*

During July or August each church school leader should receive the resources available to help him fulfill his role in the church school beginning in September, including:
- Course materials for the new semester/quarter.
- Class roll with names, addresses, telephone numbers, and birth dates of students.
- A listing of available audio-visuals (filmstrips, films, pictures, maps, etc.), including procedures for securing them for class use.
- A listing of available supplies (construction paper, pencils, scissors, etc.).
- A listing of helpful resource books in the church library related to course themes and teaching techniques.

Departmental superintendents and other administrative personnel will need similar resources.

3.) *Individual study by teachers*

Each teacher should be encouraged to study resources related to his class during the summer and at his leisure. If the retreat has already occurred, such study will continue the experience of the retreat in a setting that is more leisurely and intensive. The board or superintendent should arrange for some contact with each teacher to encourage individual study.

In some situations several teachers may be able to meet informally to study together. When needed, the pastor or director of Christian education, or the departmental superintendent or another teacher may provide individual or group consultation. Such consultation demonstrates that teaching is a team effort.

4.) *A fall planning session* is important to provide teachers with:

• an overview of the curriculum plans for the semester or quarter.

• involvement in the policy decisions of the board of Christian education.

• opportunity to work with others in exploring resources and determining teaching relationships within departments.

This planning session should be held during the two weeks prior to the first Sunday of the fall semester or quarter. The experience may be three to six hours in length. It may be scheduled for an evening, Saturday, or Sunday afternoon and evening.

One option is to plan such a session for the total teaching staff. The agenda may include worship, orientation and planning in the total group, and departmental meetings to consider age group and class concerns. A second option is several separate sessions. Leaders in various age groupings, such as children, youth, and adult, may be together; or leaders of each department may be involved in separate sessions.

Total-school concerns for a session would include an interpretation of the annual study themes of the year and plans for enrollment and promotion. Departmental meetings may be the opportunity for exploring teaching relationships and responsibilities, checking class rolls, considering telephone or other contacts with students prior to the first Sunday of the year, gathering resources, and checking on supplies.

A fall planning session may afford opportunities for last-minute consideration of details related to the effectiveness of the first sessions of classes and departments in the new church school year.

Section 5 Student Enrollment and Visitation

The emphasis upon the preparation for ministry with the learners includes the enrollment of persons in classes or groups and the planning of visitation programs to be carried out during the church school year.

ENROLLMENT OF PERSONS IN CLASSES

The annual enrollment of children, youth, and adults affords an opportunity for teachers and students to meet and to talk about forthcoming class or group learning opportunities and curriculum materials being used.

Some church school administrators and teachers are discovering that the best way to stimulate attendance is to designate a specific time at the beginning of the new church school year for enrollment in classes and groups.

The act of enrolling should be interpreted as an opportunity for individuals to enter into an agreement with school teachers, each making a commitment of intent. On the one hand, the church school makes a commitment to provide quality-level teaching-learning experiences in which persons are helped to "become aware of God" and "respond in faith and love." The learner, in turn, makes a commitment to involve himself in the life and study of a teaching-learning group.

Obviously, parents of young children will need to assume a responsibility for their enrollment. This action, however, should not be perfunctory. When children are enrolled by parents, the responsible teacher or departmental leader should make this an occasion for sharing information about curriculum content and objectives, and for stressing the importance of regular attendance.

Each church school should develop an appropriate pattern for the enrollment of students. This pattern may vary from year to year, depending upon changing circumstances. Whatever pattern is adopted, it should be regarded as an essential part of the launching of the church school year.

The following models of enrollment are worthy of consideration:

1.) *Before the fall semester begins,* on a weekday evening, a Saturday, or a Sunday afternoon. This should provide an unhurried opportunity for teachers to interpret courses of study, to acquaint students and parents with appropriate curriculum resources, to discuss teaching-learning objectives, and for learners and parents to become better acquainted with teachers and classroom settings.

2.) *During the church school hour,* in classrooms or at an "enrollment center" on one or two Sundays prior to Launch Sunday. Some churches may mail enrollment forms and a list of classes to the congregation in advance, encouraging students to devote some advance thought to the meaning and implications of enrollment.

3.) *Enrollment by mail.* This approach lacks the student-teacher involvement at the time of the enrollment. However, it has value for persons who may live at a distance, or who for other reasons cannot be present at a specified time.

4.) *Continuing enrollment.* Students who are late in enrolling or who move into the community during the church school year should be encouraged to enroll and to talk personally with the teachers about their participation in the life of the class or group. Someone can be designated to process new or late enrollments.

5.) *Another pattern.* A church may wish to select another pattern of enrollment or some combination of the above patterns. In each case, students who have been previously enrolled but fail to appear during an enrollment period should be contacted through a personal visit or telephone contact.

VISITATION PROGRAM

The importance of personal visitation in the homes of students and prospective students by teachers cannot be overemphasized. Regular visits with students *and* their families is the best way to acquire an adequate firsthand knowledge of each individual.

Visits by teachers not only establish a caring relationship with the student but provide an excellent face-to-face opportunity to discuss with families the significance of church school experiences which contribute to individual Christian growth. In addition, such contacts often result in reaching other members of the family who are not enrolled.

Of equal importance are visits by class members. Students, especially youth and adults, make a valuable witness when enlisted in the visitation of members and prospects.

Often parents of young children are willing to make calls on the families of other young children. Sometimes the parent and child may call together as official representatives of a class or department.

Teams of visitors can be formed to call in homes during a given time determined by the board of Christian education in consultation with the church school staff. Regular visitation periods, emphasized, organized, and publicized, help not only to increase interest in visitation, but also to maintain continuing pupil conversation and communication.

Visitation should be scheduled at that time of year when maximum results can be expected. In many situations the period of October and November is the best time for such a strategy because at this time enthusiasm usually runs high among teachers, students, and parents. Furthermore, additional students reached during this time are enriched by early exposure to the teaching-learning experiences of the church school year.

Purposes of the visitation. The purposes of a visitation program should be clearly stated. They may include the establishment or deepening of relationships with students, encouraging persons to participate in classes, or some other purpose. A major purpose is to acquaint a person with existing opportunities within small groups of the church school. The church will want to provide a listing of such groups, with a brief description of each one. Such a listing will be essential for a person who may be calling on individuals who are eligible for classes other than his own. The visitor may be asked to seek decisions from those visited to be involved in small groups of the church school.

Another possible purpose for visitation is to secure information concerning the interest of persons in participating in a group which presently does not exist in the church school. This feedback will suggest to the board of Christian education the possibility of establishing new groups based upon the needs and interests of the constituency.

A briefing session. Because of the significance of visitation, a briefing session for all visitors may be essential. It may be helpful to hold the session on a Sunday afternoon or early some evening, so that visitors may go from the briefing session to begin visiting. In the briefing session questions such as the following may be considered:

- What is the purpose of the visitation?
- What constitutes an effective call?
- What type of calls should be given priority?
- Which visit should be made by each visitor or visiting team?

Regular visitation. There are many advantages to an annual "crash" approach to visitation. However, this more dramatic effort should not obscure the value of regular visits by teachers and others throughout the church school year. Regular communication with pupils and calling on prospects should be stressed as basic concerns of every teacher and class.

The teacher, too? Class members and their families can express their interest in and appreciation for a teacher through a visit with the teacher. Perhaps your school can highlight a "visit your teacher" emphasis.

Section 6 Planning for Teacher Support and Training

An effective launching of the church school year includes the development of a strategy of support and training of teachers and other church school workers. The strategy is then implemented throughout the school year. The planning of such a strategy by the board of Christian education with the church school superintendent will include the determination of the objectives for the support and training efforts of the year and the scheduling of program elements which give promise of providing the support and training essential for the leaders. Such a strategy will include:

• Team building with leaders.
• Training of leaders.

TEAM BUILDING WITH LEADERS

Often a person is recruited for leadership in the church school, for example, as a teacher in a youth class, and then left to function on his own without the support of a team, without the provision for growth in his relationship to other teachers, members of the class, superintendents, or members of the board of Christian education. The only primary contact with another church school leader may be the departmental superintendent who makes a contact only when it is essential to speak about special departmental concerns.

When church school workers function as a team, they have *common or agreed upon objectives.* Team building occurs when team members experience the unique part which each person plays in assisting the group to determine its objective and to accomplish its tasks. The effectiveness of the school is enhanced by the involvement of leaders in determining the objectives.

When church school workers function as a team, there is *shared decision making.* Teachers, departmental superintendents, and others should be involved whenever possible in the making of policy and administrative decisions which directly affect their work and call for their cooperation and efforts.

When church school workers function as a team, there is *the building of relationships which afford personal encouragement and the sharing of resources.* No one can be expected to have all the

25

necessary knowledge or skills which can be utilized in the teaching-learning opportunities of a class or group. The teacher calls upon the resources of persons within the group. If he is consciously a member of a team of church school workers, he can draw upon the skills and resources of the team to support his teaching efforts. The church school superintendent is the key in the building of teams within the church school. This may indeed be one of his primary functions as liaison between the board of Christian education and the teachers and other workers of the school. He is the key leader and convener within the team of departmental superintendents. One of his functions within that team is to motivate the superintendents to work at team building on a departmental or class level.

Several ingredients may be considered for the strategy of team building for a church school year:

• The decision of the teams to be involved in team-building efforts. Participation in such efforts is dependent upon a conscious decision.

• The involvement of teachers whenever possible in the decisions which affect them.

• Informal gatherings of church school workers for the purpose of sharing and becoming acquainted.

• Scheduled team-building experiences. These may be part of other meetings, such as a retreat or an occasional session held primarily for planning or dealing with concerns. Or team-building workshops may be scheduled. Resource materials for planning team-building experiences as part of other meetings or in workshops are contained in the manual *Team Building for Church Groups,* by Nancy Geyer and Shirley Noll. (See Appendix B.)

TRAINING OF LEADERS

The concept of "teacher-learner" is that the teacher is both teacher and learner, and the student is both learner and teacher.

This concept has implications for the training of teachers. Because the teacher is a learner, his needs for learning encompass how he relates to other learners in the group, his understanding about the biblical and theological concepts of the course, and his skills related to the methods of teaching. The launching of the church school year provides the occasion for the board of Christian education through its leader development chairman to *determine its strategy for training teachers* in the coming year. The implementation of the strategy encompasses the whole school year.

In considering the training needs of teachers, one area of importance is exploration of the annual study theme or themes within the church school resources. For example, the graded resources now being used by several denominations are based upon a three-year cycle with an annual theological perspective for each year. The perspectives are: "Knowing the Living God," "Responding to God's Call to Live in Christ," and "Being the Community of Christian Love." In exploring the needs of teachers, consideration should be given to the planning of teaching-learning opportunities in which teachers may explore the annual theological theme or themes.

In determining the training strategy for the coming year, several questions should be considered. These may be looked upon as steps in the planning of a training program for the year.

What are the felt needs of your church school leaders in terms of training? New insights into their roles and relationships? An understanding of how persons learn? Skills in using the Bible? An understanding of concepts like "crossing point" or "experience-centered learning"?

What kind of training event or events should be made available? A retreat? A workshop or a series of workshops? Is it better to include all teachers or to plan events for departmental or age-group staff? Is it better to hold the event for a single congregation or to plan it for teachers of more than one church of the community? What training opportunities are available through our denomination?

When should the local church events be scheduled? Leaders should be consulted as to the best time for scheduling training events. Events should be scheduled for the time of year, the day, and hour most convenient to most teachers. When they are consulted in the planning, persons are likely to have a greater sense of commitment to participation in an event.

What resources are available? "Resources" should be interpreted to mean printed materials, audio-visuals, and persons capable of providing various kinds of training. Resources may be secured from numerous denominational and community sources. A few resources are listed in Appendix B, "Resources of Continuing Value."

What leadership should be secured? Leaders of leaders should be persons with some expertise in the area of identified need and with the ability and concern to function as both leaders and learners in training events. Such leaders are available within the congregation, the community, and denominational Christian education structures.

How may we best motivate church school leaders to participate in training events? Motivation is essential for growth in the leadership ability of church school workers. Training programs must be designed so that the growth opportunities for the trainee will be of significance to him and related to his interests, abilities, and assets. There should be study opportunities for beginners, and other types of study for more advanced teachers. A careful plan for publicity and personal promotion with teachers is essential.

RECOGNITION OF CHURCH SCHOOL WORKERS

Church school leaders devote many hours of time and effort in fulfilling their roles. They are worthy of the appreciation of those whose lives are enriched by their roles in the church's teaching ministry. The recognition of teaching staff is an essential element in the church's plan for the support of teachers. The board of Christian education should consider how to encourage such an expression of appreciation in the context of the total church and when that recognition will take place in the church school year.

Church school workers can be recognized in a number of ways. A service of recognition and dedication, such as those found in Appendix A, may be included in a congregational worship service, in a family-night program, or as part of another appropriate church occasion. A special recognition dinner for the staff, with their families as guests, may recognize the importance of the support which the staff receive from their families as they fulfill their roles. A reception or open house in classes, departments, or the total school will afford opportunities for conversation and the building of relationships between teachers, students, and their families.

An informal setting for recognition is the gathering of the teaching staff and their families in the homes of members of the board of Christian education or the board of deacons/deaconnesses.

Another option for recognition is an all-school assembly in which church school workers may be introduced and recognized. A part of the sesssion could highlight the roles and importance of the leaders.

To say "thank you" and "we appreciate you" to the teaching staff is also to give public recognition to the efforts of the board of Christian education in their support of church school workers.

Section 7 Celebrating Launch Sunday

Launch Sunday is, in effect, the kickoff of the new church school year. It may include a variety of activities designed to involve pupils, to highlight the significance of the church's educational ministry, and to create appreciation for all church school workers.

Launch Sunday is suggested for the first Sunday of the new church school year, usually in September. Because the first Sunday in September usually coincides with Labor Day weekend, serious attendance problems are created in some sections of the country. For this reason the board of Christian education, upon recommendation of the Launch Sunday Task Group, should select the best possible Sunday in September for this important event. *For most churches the second Sunday of September may be most appropriate.*

The suggested purposes for Launch Sunday are:

• to celebrate the beginning of the new church school year.

• to challenge members of the congregation to become involved in the teaching-learning experiences of the church school.

• to dramatize the significant contribution made by teachers, officers, and administrators of the church school.

There are a number of possible events for Launch Sunday including:

Enrollment. It is important to have students in classes or groups on the first Sunday of the new year. Therefore, every effort should be made for the completion of enrollment by the commencement of classes on Launch Sunday. (See Section 5.)

First meeting of church school classes. The first sessions of classes and groups will generally be held on Launch Sunday. These sessions provide an opportunity for teachers and pupils to become better acquainted, to discuss the opportunities of the year ahead, to examine the resources for the coming semester or quarter, to determine individual and group goals, and to share dreams related to the learning experiences of the coming year.

Departmental or total-school gatherings. A portion of the first church school period on Launch Sunday may be devoted to a total-school assembly or to departmental meetings. In such gatherings may be provided the opportunity for becoming better acquainted with departmental and other leaders and for considering forthcoming activities of the school or departments. Such gatherings afford the unique opportunity to celebrate the potential for learning and growth resulting from anticipated teaching-learning opportunities.

Promotion. Launch Sunday may include the promotion of students from class to class, department to department. Promotion of students is often scheduled on the first Sunday of the new church school year because summer attendance diminishes, thereby making it difficult, if not impossible, to provide meaningful teaching-learning experiences for new groupings of pupils during the summer months. When church school classes are discontinued through July and August or when teachers are absent for long periods on vacation, a Launch Sunday promotion has some distinct advantages.

Promotion should be a significant occasion for persons moving into new departments and classes. Departmental superintendents and teachers should be encouraged to extend "special greetings" to new pupils in such a way as to help them experience group acceptance at the very beginning of their relationship in new teaching-learning groups.

Corporate worship. The corporate worship experiences of the church are a natural and important arena in which to observe Launch Sunday. Celebration and commitment are significant elements in the service. In this context persons may be given the opportunity to celebrate the significance of the beginning of a new church school year and to make a commitment to the educational task of the church.

The pastor is a key person to work with the Launch Sunday Task Group to lay plans for the worship experience. More specifically, he is afforded the opportunity to plan a sermon or other presentation which will highlight the significance of the educational ministry of the church and which will challenge the congregation to participate responsibly in that ministry. Such a sermon may be based upon the current study themes of the church school. Denominations often provide resources which will be helpful to the pastor in the preparation of such a sermon.

To enable the church school leaders and the congregation to verbalize their commitment to the church's educational ministry, a litany of dedication or a service of recognition and dedication becomes a significant part of the Launch Sunday worship experience. Appendix A contains suggested resources for use in such a service.

30

Writing a litany can be a meaningful experience for a leader or student of the church school.

Recognition of church school workers may be included further in the worship context by inserting in the bulletin a list of teaching personnel and their specific responsibilities. Such a listing may serve to highlight the significance of the church school within the context of the church's total ministry and to indicate the teaching-learning groups available in the school.

Another possibility for the Launch Sunday service is the inclusion of a verbal statement or statements by students concerning the significance of the teaching-learning opportunities for them. Some churches may wish to include a slide or other visual presentation to highlight the life and ministry of the church school.

Informal reception for church school workers. The congregation may be given the opportunity to express appreciation to the staff of the school in an informal reception on Launch Sunday. A reception line and light refreshments will enhance the experience. Such a reception may be held at the close of the worship service or between the service and the church school, depending on the church's Sunday morning schedule.

Open house. An "open house" may provide an informal opportunity for persons to visit in the classrooms of other members of the family or of friends. It provides an occasion for conversation between teachers and visitors. Open house may be held during a part of the church school hour, between the church school sessions and the worship service, or following the worship hour, again depending on the church's Sunday schedule and other planned Launch Sunday events.

The possible events for Launch Sunday are numerous. The key task may not be so much in discovering the possible events as in selecting and scheduling those events which promise to be most significant to the congregation in a given year.

Section 8 Responsibility of the Board

The manner in which the board approaches the annual Launch can make a tremendous difference in the "enthusiasm level" of the congregation, the response of church school teachers and students, and the success of launch events.

Obviously it is not the responsibility of the board to design every educational event, but to make certain that adequate planning, designing, and staffing is done by selected board members or by other competent persons. In relation to the annual Launch such questions as the following need to be examined:

- Who will administer the events of the Launch?
- Which events should the board design?
- Who will plan, administer, and staff Launch Sunday events?
- How can the annual Launch be made a total church concern?
- What additional leadership is needed?

Some aspects of the Launch must, of necessity, be the responsibility of the board acting as "a committee of the whole." These aspects include determining objectives and policy for the church school year, planning some events such as the retreat for church school staff and board members, and planning the strategy for acquainting the congregation with the school.

The chairman of the board will take the initiative in such planning, and basic planning should begin as early as the February board meeting if possible.

Delegation of responsibility is necessary in order to enlist additional competent persons for leadership, as well as to obtain new and creative ideas from persons not normally involved in program designing. Committees and task groups ought to be chosen, assignments made, and opportunities provided for periodic feedback, sharing, and evaluating by the board.

Responsibility for several events should be delegated to the church school superintendent and to other persons who are in the most advantageous position to work directly with students, parents, and family groups. The superintendent and others may be asked to design events related to the recruitment and preparation of leaders, enrollment, and visitation (Sections 4 and 5). The leader development chairman of the board may be designated to develop the strategy for teacher support and training (Section 6).

Having delegated this responsibility, the board will look to the superintendent to convene the task group. The task group will formulate plans, schedule events, select leadership, initiate publicity, and report regularly concerning developments.

The coordination of launch emphases is a task which ought to be assumed by the board itself. Only this group is capable of viewing the Launch in "total perspective." Care must be taken to keep all elements "in balance" so that the program does not become unmanageable, and thereby ineffective.

Plans being made for the Launch by board members and by the task group should be shared month-by-month, beginning in March, more frequently if possible. This review will avoid duplication of effort, inadequate leadership enlistment, and unrealistic expectations of teachers and students.

In summary, the board assumes responsibility for the total Launch, designing some events itself, and delegating responsibility for other events to qualified persons.

Section 9 Role of the Church School Superintendent

It is essential that the church school be administered by a competent person, working in close cooperation with the board in order to insure a program of quality Christian education, the continuing involvement of teachers and department leaders, as well as the response of students from week to week. Thus, the general superintendent functions as a key person in relation to all programs or events involving the church school.

No leader in the church's educational ministry is more advantageously situated than the church school superintendent to serve as a liaison between the board of Christian education and the church school teaching staff. This role and relationship alone, assuming other necessary organizational and administrative abilities, admirably qualifies the superintendent for serious consideration as chairman of the Launch Sunday Task Group.

The designing of Launch Sunday should be carried out by the superintendent in collaboration with the three age-group chairmen and the pastor, functioning as the Launch Sunday Task Group. The age-group chairmen, related to the church's educational ministry with children, youth, and adults, generally are not only personally acquainted with teachers and students, but have firsthand knowledge of leadership resources that might contribute to the success of Launch Sunday.

This task group should be delegated by the board to design Launch Sunday, select leadership, calendar the various events, and to see that adequate publicity is prepared. Suggested Launch Sunday events are described in Section 7.

Obviously, plans and programs being projected should be shared with the board at regular intervals for review and approval in order to keep them in proper perspective and in harmony with overall plans for the total Launch.

Occupying the spotlight of leadership in designing and administering Launch Sunday emphases, the church school superintendent ought to approach this assignment with a high degree of enthusiasm and expectation, comparable to the enthusiastic planning invested in previous "Rally Day" programs. Actually, Launch Sunday contains many ingredients similar to those of Rally Day.

Given the same fervent promotion, Launch Sunday can result in meaningful experiences for students promoted to new classes, for members of groups as they anticipate exciting teaching-learning experiences in the months ahead, for families as they sense anew the importance of Christian teaching for every member, for teachers as they look forward to deeply significant and challenging class sessions each week, and for members of the congregation as they may acquire a new understanding or appreciation of Christian education ministry.

In the final analysis, the success of Launch Sunday depends in no small measure upon the esprit-de-corps and team effort of the general superintendent, board members, departmental leaders, members of the teaching staff, and the pastor. Throughout all of the planning, designing, dialoguing, staffing, and scheduling, the superintendent's leadership, catalytic influence, and administrative supervision should be evident, thereby maintaining morale, providing support and encouragement, keeping everyone apprised of goals and objectives, and creating a contagious climate of enthusiasm and expectancy.

It is obvious that Launch Sunday represents only "a beginning" of each new church school year. The mobilization of teachers, the heightened enthusiasm level of students, the recognition of Christian education workers, and the response of church members should motivate every church school superintendent to conserve as well as to build upon these assets. Immediate follow-up plans and strategies ought to be developed for increasing the attendance of students at every age level, the continuing follow-up of absentees, visitation in the homes of students, and additional enrichment opportunities for teachers in the church school. The alert and sensitive superintendent will not relax when Launch Sunday has passed, but will continue to engender a growing spirit of cooperation, enthusiasm, and commitment throughout the church school.

Section 10 Role of the Pastor

The pastor is a key person in the church's educational ministry. His training and full-time position, often as the only full-time staff person in the church, make him a logical leader in the educational ministry. Much of the vitality of that ministry stems from the leadership which the pastor exerts.

If there is a second minister on the church staff, such as a director or minister of Christian education, there is a pastoral team. Whether two or more, all members of the team have relationships and responsibilities in education and in the other ministries of the church, though in varying roles depending on job descriptions. In many churches the director or minister of Christian education assumes primary responsibility for the overall administration of the annual Launch.

Even though primary educational functions are delegated to a director or minister of Christian education, the pastor or senior minister should maintain a supporting and counseling relationship in the educational program, including the church school. He should continue to be involved in and informed of the objectives, needs, and concerns of the school.

Whether the pastor serves alone or as a member of a pastoral team in the church, there are significant ways in which he can contribute to the effectiveness of the annual launching of the church school year:

His role as *consultant to the board of Christian education* may be very significant. He may help the board in its efforts to formulate the objectives for the church school, to determine and plan launch events, and to select leadership.

The Launch Sunday Task Group, under the leadership of the church school superintendent, *may benefit from the assistance of the pastor as consultant and resource person.* The pastor has a significant role in the planning of appropriate worship experiences for Launch Sunday. His leadership will be essential in the planning of a sermon or presentation to highlight educational ministry, a dedication of church school workers, and the inclusion in the worship service of other elements to motivate enthusiasm for the ministry of the school. (See Section 7.)

Many pastors include in their preaching plan for the year sermons related to educational themes and emphases. Such a series in the fall may enhance the launching of the church school year. One pastor led his church to accept a book describing the current study themes of the church school as the Book of the Year for the church. On the third Sunday of each month the sermon was related to the study themes. Following the service, a "sermon-reflection" opportunity was scheduled for discussion of the sermon topic. The congregation was invited to purchase the book and to enter into the year's cooperative study.

In one community the American Baptist, the Disciples, and the Church of God pastors adopted similar sermon themes and topics from the annual study book which was basic to the church school resources being used in each church. The pastors met weekly during September and October to discuss the common topic and sermon ideas each would use the following Sunday.

The pastor is often described as the "teacher of teachers." One way to fulfill this description is to serve as a leader of a study group or groups of teachers who are exploring the theological themes inherent within the church school resources of a given year. The pastor's relationship to the teaching staff may afford him opportunities for counseling with teachers and administrators of the school regarding theological and biblical concerns. Pastoral contacts will afford many opportunities for informal visits and for letters urging persons to enroll in classes or groups of the church school.

The pastor is quite often the person most strategically able to keep the congregation informed about the church school—its program, needs, objectives, and accomplishments. The worship bulletin and the worship service itself are two important media for fulfilling this function.

The alert pastor will be perceptive to the feedback which comes to him from the congregation regarding the leadership and teaching-learning opportunities of the church school. The sensitivity to such feedback and his helpful and tactful sharing of this feedback with the church school superintendent and board of Christian education offer promise of strengthening the effectiveness of the school.

Without the support and active participation of the pastor, the launching of the church school year will lack some of the vitality which it needs. With his full participation, added vitality may be present.

Section 11 Involving the Church School Staff

The entire church school staff has an investment in the annual Launch. The time and personal effort spent by teachers during the launching of the church school year are certain to return larger dividends in student enrollment, to create a climate of trust and acceptance among students and teachers, and to evoke enthusiastic responses from parents and family groups.

Teachers should be helped to appreciate the Launch as an occasion for individual preparation, enrichment, and theological orientation, as well as a time to reinforce bonds of understanding and personal relationship with class and department members.

Early in the planning process for the annual Launch, the chairman of the board, the church school superintendent, and the Launch Sunday Task Group should meet with teachers and departmental superintendents in an unhurried session for the purpose of encouraging suggestions and of discussing the feasibility and value of each launch event.

Such a meeting has psychological as well as practical value. Most church school teachers seldom participate in basic decision making which affects the total life of the church school. Not only do teachers and officers possess valuable insights and program ideas, but also they are capable of creative implementation as well as supportive leadership. The enlistment and counsel of these co-workers at an early point in the planning process can spell the difference between success and failure in reaching large numbers of students and families through the church's teaching ministry.

In orientation sessions, church school workers should become acquainted with every aspect of the Launch, thereby assessing their individual roles and involvement in the total Launch. These key leaders should be motivated to the point that they are willing to make the Launch a "personal top-priority" during the period of June through October.

The Task Group or the superintendent should help teachers and officers to identify and understand each launch emphasis and event, as well as the value of each for every church school worker.

It is far wiser for the board and the superintendent to acquaint church school staff members with the entire spectrum of launch events, soliciting their cooperation and concurrence, than to choose arbitrarily specific emphases that may not evoke the leadership support of these important colleagues.

Having provided this initial orientation, continuing contacts with the church school staff should be made by the general superintendent and department superintendents. The enthusiasm and continuing involvement of teachers can best be maintained through personal weekly contacts.

The general superintendent and church school workers should schedule regular meetings prior to and during the Launch in order to reinforce each other and to give attention to the implementation of each launch event. Department superintendents should also be encouraged to have dialogue with their respective teachers from week to week so that the full impact and value of the Launch is experienced by students at every age level.

Church school workers may favor different emphases in the annual Launch from those initiated and approved by the board. In such cases, their suggestions and recommendations should be transmitted to the board by the general superintendent. The board, in turn, should give these proposals careful consideration, assessing their feasibility in relation to overall launch objectives. Board decisions related to suggestions received from church school workers ought to be "reported back" immediately, along with an "explanatory rationale" whenever the board concludes that other projects or programs ought to receive priority attention.

In the final analysis, no one in the entire church has a more direct relationship to or exerts more influence upon students than do teachers and department superintendents. Of all who serve as leaders in the church, these dedicated men and women make the greatest investment of time and talent in Christian nurture and education. As teachers, they carry the sobering responsibility of interpreting and transmitting the faith week after week to children, youth, and adults.

The enthusiasm and dedicated commitment of these key leaders to the task of Christian teaching needs both reinforcement and support from time to time. For this reason, the observance of the annual Launch is invaluable in helping to provide fresh incentives for teachers, a new perspective upon the significance of teaching ministry, renewed vigor of mind and spirit, and more clearly defined personal goals and expectations. Such renewal on the part of teachers and other church school workers is certain to have its effect upon the response of students at every age level.

Section 12 Involving the Congregation

The annual Launch should be regarded as a churchwide emphasis, focusing attention upon the importance of Christian teaching-learning experiences for every member of the congregation.

Special plans need to be made in order to engender congregational interest, enthusiasm, support, and commitment. In making such plans the board, or a task force, should explore every possible means of "bringing the congregation on board." The purpose of this publicity and promotion is to enlist congregational support of the Launch, to enroll more persons in classes or groups, and to create an increasing awareness of and commitment to the church's teaching ministry as it touches persons of all ages.

The involvement of the pastor is vitally important in enlisting desired congregational support and response. Whoever administers the annual Launch should work closely with the pastor in making certain that plans and expectations are realistic, that members are acquainted with the purpose and significance of the Launch, that a good "climate" of acceptance is being created, and that everything possible is done to make this event a never-to-be-forgotten experience.

Some Launch Sunday events are especially designed to attract the interest, attendance, and participation of the entire congregation. Adequately planned and publicized, these emphases can provide inspiration, enrichment, and a new sense of belonging to a deeply significant fellowship. Those who plan the events of this day should be aware of the importance of publicizing and promoting churchwide attendance.

The following promotional techniques have proven valuable in the interpretation and promotion of the annual Launch:

• *Personal letters to members of the church school staff* from the chairman of the board, church school superintendent, or pastor, inviting them to participate in certain launch events and to regard these events as "top priority" commitments. This type of communication not only helps each worker to envision the total scope of the Launch, but also to identify specific emphases in which the worker has a high investment of interest. In addition, "the personal touch" is often invaluable in enlisting the support of co-workers.

40

- *Letters to church members and church school students* from the pastor, possibly one in July and a second in August, describing the objectives of the Launch with special emphasis upon Launch Sunday.
- *The inclusion of notices in the church bulletin* during the summer months, leading up to Launch Sunday. Notices are valuable in establishing a climate of anticipation and receptivity throughout the congregation. Some novel or innovative method of calling attention to specific events and to individuals or groups involved in them may well be used.
- *Attractive posters or banners hung where they can be clearly seen.* These will add a visual dimension to the promotion of launch events. Children and youth in the church school, as well as adults having artistic skill, might be enlisted for this type of promotional material. Special attention can be drawn by having students present banners in the worship services during the weeks preceding Launch Sunday.
- *Class/department announcements by teachers and departmental superintendents,* along with telephone calls to church school students, beginning in early August. Such techniques will not only reflect the personal interest of leaders in their students, but also begin to establish person-to-person relationships upon which subsequent teaching-learning experiences will be built. Often personal contacts and telephone conversations will do more to arouse interest and to enlist support than any other single effort.
- *Enthusiastic public announcements by the pastor.* These are certain to establish a climate of expectancy among church members. The board or task force might prepare a series of spot announcements for the pastor's guidance in mentioning the Launch in services of worship. Combined with other efforts being made to interpret the significance of the Launch and to enlist more persons in the church's teaching ministry, the verbal endorsement of the pastor provides added incentive for some members who might otherwise remain indifferent.

Bringing the congregation on board represents more than increasing attendance on Launch Sunday. It really means that the board and others responsible for planning will make a serious effort to involve personally as many individuals as possible in their support of the church's educational ministry through participation in teaching-learning groups, systematic reading and study, leadership in age-group programs, and a deeper commitment to quality Christian teaching for persons at every age level.

Appendix A Suggestions for Dedication Services

SERVICE OF RECOGNITION AND DEDICATION OF CHURCH SCHOOL WORKERS

We have gathered as a congregation not only to worship God and to experience again the joys of Christian fellowship, but also to recognize a staff of dedicated persons who contribute significant leadership in the educational ministry of our church.

Planning, administering, and serving as leaders and teachers of children, youth, and adults necessitates the investment of valuable time, discipline in preparation, and personal commitment to the church's teaching ministry.

We take this opportunity to express appreciation to all who serve as teachers, church school officers, and members of the board of Christian education. This service of dedication provides an opportunity for these leaders to reaffirm their commitment to educational ministry, as well as for the entire congregation to express gratitude, prayerful support, and concern for a continuing program of quality Christian education. Let us now join in such an affirmation.

Congregational Commitment
(Remaining seated)

Minister: For these who by precept and example have lighted the pathways of children, youth, and adults in their spiritual growth,
Congregation: We thank thee, O God.
Minister: For these who have taught with love and joy and patience,
Congregation: We thank thee, O God.
Minister: For these who have had the larger vision of the kingdom of God, and who have given time and talent to the one increasing purpose of establishing it on earth,
Congregation: We thank thee, O God.
Minister: For all who have, in other days, spent their lives in consecrated service that this church might minister to the spiritual needs of this community and share in the Christian world mission,
Congregation: We thank thee, O God.

Officers, Teachers, and Board Members
(Standing as they participate)

Minister: You who stand in the presence of this company have been chosen to a sacred trust. Do you individually commit yourselves anew to the teaching ministry of our church?

Response: We do.

Minister: You have been called by the Master Teacher to follow in his steps. To the holy task and high privilege of Christian teaching, we commission you anew.

Response: We accept the call to service and the challenge of our task. We acknowledge the sacredness of our mission of guiding and nourishing the lives of those entrusted by God to our care. We believe that we are fulfilling the plan of God for the extension of his kingdom, and will be sincere in our dedication and trustworthy in our task.

Minister: To you has been entrusted a task that requires vision of goals ahead, faith to believe that the will of God can be done, and knowledge of how to attain high educational objectives. To the fulfillment of these obligations, do you dedicate yourselves today?

Response: We dedicate the best of our abilities and skills, and pledge ourselves to use the full powers of our hands, our minds, and our hearts in undertaking these, our sacred responsibilities.

Congregational Response
(All standing together)

Minister: As members and friends of our church, as students in our church school, as parents of children and youth, to you has been entrusted an important responsibility in our task of Christian teaching and spiritual nurture. Without your loyal support, prayers, sympathetic understanding, and active attendance, we cannot carry on successfully this important Christian enterprise. We now ask you to acknowledge your share in this task.

Congregation: Realizing our share in building the kingdom of God, we pledge our wholehearted cooperation to those to whom we have entrusted responsibility for leadership in the spiritual development of children, youth, and adults. We consecrate our lives, our money, and our prayers to the support of this task of Christian education in our church. Amen.

A LITANY OF DEDICATION FOR LAUNCH SUNDAY

ASCRIPTION

Pastor: O God, upon whose precepts and gracious love the foundations of the world are established,

People: To Thee we give our love, O Lord.

Pastor: Lord Jesus, founder of our faith and head of the church, who has commanded us to preach and teach whatsoever you have taught us,

People: To Thee we give our loyalty, O Christ.

Pastor: O Holy Spirit, given to be our abiding teacher who gives us gifts to be used in thy service,

People: To Thee we dedicate our lives, O God.

THE WORD

Pastor: "Remember also your Creator in the days of your youth."

People: "The Lord gives wisdom; from his mouth come knowledge and understanding."

Pastor: "Keep hold of instruction, do not let go; guard her, for she is your life."

People: "Do your best to present yourself to God as one approved . . . rightly handling the word of truth."

PRAYER IN UNISON

O God, who through the prophets teaches men your way and will, we rejoice that your voice has not grown silent. Give us teachers to lead us into your truth and to train us for ministry in your kingdom—through Jesus Christ our great teacher, we pray. Amen.

THANKSGIVING

Pastor: In this day which begins a new church school year, with its prospect of new discoveries and new life,

People: We rejoice, O Lord.

Pastor: For teachers and learners growing together,

People: We thank Thee, our Father.

Pastor: For new resources, prepared by dedicated educators under your guidance,

People: We thank Thee, our Father.

Pastor: For ministries of reconciliation in the world, and for the training that makes us good ministers of Jesus Christ,

People: We thank Thee, our Father.

Pastor: For the gathering of your people to give thanks for the past and to prepare for the future,

People: We rejoice, O Lord.

DEDICATION

Pastor: To the task and joy of guiding children and youth,

People: Let all parents be dedicated, O Lord.

Pastor: To the teaching of your law and your love,

People: Let all teachers in the church school be dedicated, O Lord.

Pastor: To the living of your word, that the inside man and the outside man may tell the same story,

People: Let all members of the congregation be dedicated, O Lord.

Pastor: To be participants and not just observers in the teaching ministry of the church,

People: We dedicate ourselves, O Lord.

PRAYER IN UNISON

Give to us open minds, that your truth may not be hindered by cloudy thinking or unholy love of self.

Give us loving hearts, that we may enter creatively into the lives of those we teach.

Grant us sensitive spirits, that we may hear the questions that others ask, and seek answers with patience and love.

In all of our work in the church and in the world this year, enable us to work cheerfully as partners in Christ. Amen.

Appendix B Resources of Continuing Value

ADMINISTRATION

Cober, Kenneth L., *The Church's Teaching Ministry*. Valley Forge: Judson Press, 1964. A resource for administrators, teachers, and other leaders in the church's educational ministry.

Cober, Kenneth L., *Shaping the Church's Educational Ministry*. Valley Forge: Judson Press, 1971. A manual for the board or committee of Christian education, considering the philosophy, structures, planning, administration, and resources of the educational ministry of the church.

CHURCH SCHOOL

Lynn, Robert W., and Wright, Elliott, *The Big Little School*. New York: Harper & Row, Publishers, 1971. A study of "two hundred years of the Sunday school," considering its inner working and bureaucracies and its impact on other American institutions.

Sandt, Eleanor E., *Variations on the Sunday Church School*. New York: The Seabury Press, Inc., 1967. Reports of actual experiences in churches throughout the country that have resulted in more rewarding Christian education.

Westerhoff, John H., *Values for Tomorrow's Children*. Philadelphia: Pilgrim Press, imprint of United Church Press, 1970. A look at the entire church as a community of faith involved in learning, and a call to develop new educational patterns as alternatives to the traditional Sunday church school hour.

CHURCH SCHOOL SUPERINTENDENT

Jones, Idris, *The Superintendent Plans His Work*. Valley Forge: Judson Press, 1956. A practical guide for the church school superintendent.

Keckley, Weldon, *The Church School Superintendent* (The Person and the Job). St. Louis: The Bethany Press, 1963. A consideration of the person, relationships, and roles of the church school superintendent.

PERSPECTIVE BOOKS AND GUIDES

Ashbrook, James B., *be/come COMMUNITY*. Valley Forge: Judson Press, 1971. An interpretation of Perspective III, "Being the Community of Christian Love."

Cober, Kenneth L., *Guide for Group Use for be/come Community*. Valley Forge: American Baptist Board of Education and Publication, 1971. A leader's guide for groups studying *be/come COMMUNITY*.

Becker, Edwin, *Responding to God's Call*. Valley Forge: American Baptist Board of Education and Publication, 1970. An interpretation of Perspective II, "Responding to God's Call to Live in Christ."

Remick, Oscar, *Guide for Group Use for Responding to God's Call.* Valley Forge: American Baptist Board of Education and Publication, 1970. A leader's guide for groups studying *Responding to God's Call.*

Hazelton, Roger, *Knowing the Living God.* Valley Forge: Judson Press, 1969. An interpretation of Perspective I, "Knowing the Living God."

Garrett, Cyril D., *Guide for Group Use for Knowing the Living God.* Valley Forge: American Baptist Board of Education and Publication, 1969. A leader's guide for groups studying *Knowing the Living God.*

TEACHING-LEARNING

Ban, Joseph, *Education for Change.* Valley Forge: Judson Press, 1968. An interpretation of the philosophy and theology of the Christian Faith and Work Plan, a curriculum plan based on the interdenominational Cooperative Curriculum Project.

Clark, M. Edward, *Guide for Group Use for Education for Change.* Valley Forge: American Baptist Board of Education and Publication, 1968. A leader's guide for groups studying *Education for Change.*

TRAINING AND SUPPORT OF TEACHERS

An annual packet of resources is prepared for the Focus on the Teaching Ministry, a teacher-training program, by the American Baptist Board of Education and Publication. These resources from previous Focus Packets are of continuing value for teaching training and support within a church:

Clark, M. Edward, *Experience-Centered Learning for Church Leaders.* Valley Forge: American Baptist Board of Education and Publication, 1970. Resources for planning teaching-learning sessions on experience-centered learning for teachers and other church leaders. Supportive resources: resource sheets "Biblical Foundations" by M. Edward Clark (one per participant); resource sheets "Training in Christianity" by Soren Kierkegaard (one per participant); and 1970 Focus Record (available from Division of Educational Ministries, ABBEP, Valley Forge, Pa. 19481).

Crossing Point. A thirty-minute color film designed to introduce the basic educational-theological concept of the curriculum through a thought-provoking, discussion-starter drama (available through city, state, and regional Christian education offices of the American Baptist Convention).

Geyer, Nancy, and Noll, Shirley, *Team Building in Church Groups.* Valley Forge: Judson Press, 1970. Resource manual for planning "team building" experiences to help church groups function more effectively as teams.

Focus Workshop Resources, designed for leaders of teaching-learning workshops for church school leaders (available from Division of Educational Ministries, ABBEP, Valley Forge, Pa. 19481):

1.) *The Teacher as Person.* A guide; "1969 Focus Record"; and a poster "The Role of the Teacher." To help teachers define their role and consider how their responses to persons, ideas, and situations affect that role.

2.) *The Teacher and "Meanings and Experiences."* A guide; "1969 Focus Record." To help teachers to distinguish between the knowledge and experience of "meanings and experiences" and to recognize those which persons bring to learning situations.

3.) *The Teacher and the Learning Tasks.* A guide; 7 poster-like diagrams. To help teachers recognize how persons learn and change.

4.) *The Teacher and the Biblical Message.* A guide; a 16-page *Baptist Leader* reprint "The Use of the Bible in the Christian Faith and Work Plan" (one per participant). To consider and experience the use of the Bible in teaching-learning situations.

5.) *The Teacher and Evaluation.* A guide, to enable teachers to have a working knowledge of and plans for the process of evaluation.